AF447998

Acknowledgment

The concept for storytelling to empower
the immune system was suggested to me
by my wife Pauline. She recalled a
television programme that demonstrated
the enhancement of antibodies in children
of four to five years, after they had viewed
a specific cartoon.

Using my knowledge of Guided Imagery
and Pauline's experience as a children's
nurse, this story was devised to empower
young children receiving chemotherapy to
enhance the effect of the treatment and
strengthen their immune system.

Once upon a time, there was a wonderful Kingdom called Bodi. This Kingdom was ruled by a very clever person called King Brain.

Everyone in the Kingdom liked
King Brain and they obeyed his
Royal orders because they
knew he was a good person
and was very clever.

The King had his soldiers to serve and protect his country and his people from being attacked by outside invaders. He had a Red army and a White army.

The Red army had no
weapons as their job was to
carry very special foods to all
parts of the Kingdom of Bodi.

The White army was the
fighting army, it was strong
and had lots of weapons to
help then keep out the
enemies of the King.

The Kingdom of Bodi had been a peaceful place for such a long time that whilst the Red army worked very hard, the White army had very little to do and became lazy.

This laziness became known
to those outside the Kingdom
and one day some evil invaders
planned an attack on the
Kingdom of Bodi.

The invaders started to take
over the Kingdom of Bodi and
all the people in the villages
began to suffer.

These invaders thought that
they could secretly capture
the soldiers of the White
Army one at a time and take
their weapons away.

They thought that no one
would notice the soldiers slowly
disappearing and they would be
able to take over the Kingdom
without a big fight.

Although King Brain was a clever person, he was a very busy King taking care of the Kingdom and he did not know that his White army was being attacked until he called on them to fight

and realised it had become
quite small and weak because
a lot of the weapons had
been taken away and the
soldiers were tired.

The King was very unhappy
at hearing his people being
treated badly, so he went to
see his powerful magician
Merlin.

He told Merlin that he needed
a powerful magic potion that
would help his white army

grow stronger and stronger,
more strong than they had
ever been, so that they could
destroy the invaders.

Merlin worked hard on the
magic potion until he was able
to make enough for all the
soldiers to have some.

When King Brain got this magic potion, he asked Merlin to cast a spell on him to make him invisible to all the invaders and was then able to secretly give the potion to all the soldiers in his army.

After all the soldiers had taken the potion the felt tired for a few hours and then became like incredible hulks and a great battle started.

Biff *** Bash ***

Biff *** Bash ***

went the soldiers, until all the
invaders had been destroyed.

Once again, the Kingdom of
Bodi was at peace and happy.
King Brain gave Merlin the
highest honour in the land and
promised his people that never
again would they be
threatened by the invaders.

To make sure his promise was kept, he visited all his armies every week to see that they had all that was necessary to keep them on the alert.

And the whole of the Kingdom
of Bodi lived happily ever
after.